# Auntie's

## Book of Memories

## For my Niece

©Traditions Press, Inc.

Designed and illustrated by n s taylor

Auntie's Book of Memories for My Niece

ISBN: 9781079954098

www.traditionspress.com

For Wendy and all the wonderful Aunties!

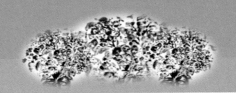

Memories

for my precious

Niece

_____

from

Aunt

_____

Date_____

Come and Listen,

My Little One,

And I will tell you stories

of when I was Young.


On a bench in the garden,

Or as we sit by the sea,

We have stories to share,

just You and Me.

Special Photo of Us

# Letter to My Niece

family photos

# My Family History

(nickname)_____

Full name

_____

Date and place of birth

_____

Occupation

_____

My parents

My Mother _____

Dates _____

Occupation: _____


My Father _____

Dates _____

Occupation: _____

Where I grew up and what
life was like when I was a child...

# Schooling

Elementary:

Middle:

High School:

And Beyond:

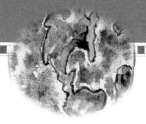

# Favorite Places & Travels

# People who inspire me

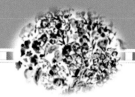

# Favorites

My favorite color    _____

My favorite flower    _____.

The best cookies are    _____.

Favorite Pets    _____.

Favorite place to visit _____.

Best friend_____

Favorite birthday_____

Favorite teacher_____

## Other Favorites

_____

_____

_____

_____

_____

_____

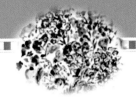

# Books, Movies & Entertainment

## Favorite Movies

## Favorite Television Show

## Favorite Songs

## Favorite Books

## Favorite Artist

# Words of Wisdom for My Niece

Quote:_____
_____
_____
_____
Attributed to _____

Quote:_____
_____
_____
_____
Attributed to _____

Quote:_____
_____
_____
_____
Attributed to _____

# Words of Wisdom for My Niece

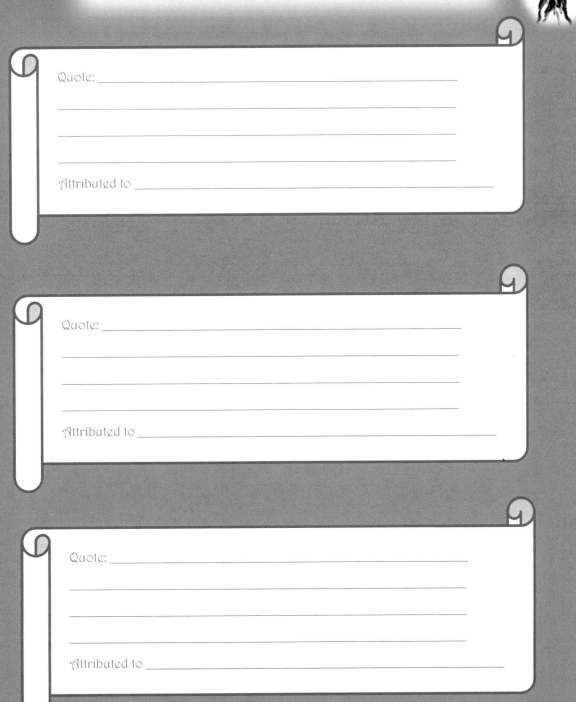

Quote: _____

_____

_____

_____

Attributed to _____

Quote: _____

_____

_____

_____

Attributed to _____

Quote: _____

_____

_____

_____

Attributed to _____

# Inventions and discoveries that
# happened during my lifetime

# Major Historical Events
# during my lifetime

# Activities and Hobbies

# Family Stories & Traditions

Special times we have shared together

Special times we have shared together

Special times we have shared together

Special times we have shared together

photos and mementos

photos & mementos

photos and mementos

photos & mementos

photos and mementos

My Love and Wishes for You

Sing and Dance,

Laugh and Play.

And Fall In Love

with Every Day!

Made in the USA
Middletown, DE
09 May 2020